CHINA

CHINA

MAO'S REPUBLIC TO WORLD SUPERPOWER

LIGHTNING
GUIDES

For general information on our other products
and services or to obtain technical support, please
contact our Customer Care Department within the
United States at (866) 744-2665, or outside the
United States at (510) 253-0500.

Lightning Guides publishes its books in a variety
of electronic and print formats. Some content that
appears in print may not be available in electronic
books, and vice versa.

ISBN Print 978-1-942411-48-2
eBook 978-1-942411-49-9

Front Cover Photo: ICHIRO/Getty Images
Back Cover Photo: ZHONG/Getty Images
Interior Photos: Zheng Long/Stocksy, p.1; Gavin
Hellier/Stocksy, p.2; Matteo Colombo, p.5;
redstone/Shutterstock, p.6; Mick Ryan/Getty
Images, p.7; VLADJ55/Shutterstock, p.9; Kajdi
Szabolcs/iStock, p.9; Sfio Cracho/Shutterstock,
p.9; [Public domain]/Wikimedia Commons, p.13;
Everett Historical/Shutterstock, p.14; BERIT
ROALD/AFP/Getty Images, p.15; Everett Historical/
Shutterstock, p.17; © Lin Yiguang/Xinhua Press/
CORBIS, p.19; maxhorng/Shutterstock, p.20; Apic/
Getty Images, p.22; Ivan Pavlov/Shutterstock,
p.23; E guoqing – Imaginechina/Associated Press,
p.27; AGIP/RDA/Hulton Archive/Getty Images,
p. 28; fourb/Shutterstock, p.31; ASSOCIATED
PRESS, p.32; © The Dmitri Baltermants Collection/
CORBIS, p.36; neelsky/Shutterstock, p.38,39;
zhang kan,/Shutterstock, p.39; © Iain Masterton/
Alamy, p.41; David Hume Kennerly [Public domain]
Wikimedia Commons, p.42; © trianide/iStock,
p.45; Karen Su/Getty Images, p.47; © Pictorial
Press Ltd/Alamy, p.49; © AF archive/Alamy, p.50;
NASA [Public domain] /Wikimedia Commons, p.53;
© Bettmann/CORBIS, p.55; Kevin Frayer/Getty
Images, p.63; Vittoriano Rastelli/Corbis, p.64; Curt
Smith/Flickr, p.66, p.67; Justin Sullivan/Getty Images,
p.68; © Grant Delin/Corbis Outline, p.69; BEN
STANSALL/AFP/Getty Images, p.70; JOERG KOCH/
AFP/Getty Images, p.71; PHILIPPE LOPEZ/AFP/
Getty Images, p.73; R.M. Nunes/Shutterstock.com,
p.75; JHPhoto/Alamy, p.76; Philippe Roy/Getty
Images, p.78; © Corbis, p.80; © Imaginechina/
Corbis, p.83; ADA_photo/Shutterstock, p.83; Mauro
Pezzotta/Shutterstock, p.83; cozyta/Shutterstock,
p.83; Yang yang – Imaginechina/Associated
Press, p.84,85; Wang lixin – Imaginechina/
Associated Press, p.87; NotarYES/Shutterstock,
p.88; coloursinmylife/Shutterstock, p.91; [Public
domain]/Wikimedia Commons, p.92; ASSOCIATED
PRESS, p. 94,95; Wang zhou – Imaginechina/
Associated Press, p.97; © China/Alamy, p.98

"In waking a tiger, use a long stick."

—MAO ZEDONG

Like China itself, Mao is complex and contradictory. His reforms led to the end of imperialism and the rapid modernization of China. He promoted the status of women, improved education and healthcare, and planted the seeds of a modern superpower. He was a poet, a theorist, a brilliant military strategist, and a visionary. Along the way, he was responsible for almost 70 million deaths through execution, starvation, and forced labor—more people were killed under Mao's rule than under any other government in history. Today China remains a mix of contradictions. In rural China, farmers lead lives that have not changed in hundreds of years, while Shanghai is literally sinking under the weight of new construction. Eight hundred years after Genghis Khan ruled the largest empire in history, the Middle Kingdom is once again taking center stage—a world military and economic superpower, she is a force to be reckoned with.

CONTENTS

This gigantic, sprawling land of a billion people has engaged the imagination and curiosity of the West for centuries. Much of this curiosity, sadly, has been in the form of offensive misconceptions: China as a mysterious land, both tantalizing and menacing. Chinese immigrants, arriving in the United States in the 19th century, were branded as "celestials"—a people so unfamiliar as to have sprung from another planet, in the assumptions and narrow-minded views of Westerners whose own ancestors had immigrated to the United States not long before.

China's past and present are as diverse and dynamic as the individuals who shape it, and while the country has seen tragedy, it has also seen triumph—it is a fount of art, culture, education, theology, technology, and inventions (paper, silk, the compass, the first standardized currency and measurements). In the past few decades, it has emerged as a global superpower and economic giant.

China has used its massive economic heft to increase its political influence around the globe, making diplomatic and economic inroads in Africa, North America, and elsewhere. Its emergence has also raised human-rights concerns about a harsh, repressive rule over Tibet and political and cultural suppression within China itself.

Global politics move at warp speed, and it's impossible to predict the future accurately. But this rising superpower will only continue to make its presence felt. The effects of China's growing dominance and how the United States interprets and responds to it are an open question. A new, confident China has arrived on the world stage.

FIRST, A FEW FACTS

CHINA'S OFFICIAL NAME IS
ZHONGHUA RENMIN GONGHE GUO
PEOPLE'S REPUBLIC OF CHINA

CHINA FALLS WITHIN
ONE TIME ZONE
IN SOME PLACES SUNRISE IS
10AM

CHINA'S LARGEST ETHNIC GROUP IS THE
HAN
who make up
92%
OF THE POPULATION

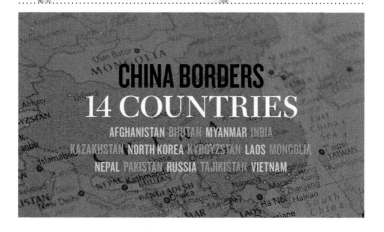

CHINA BORDERS
14 COUNTRIES

AFGHANISTAN BHUTAN MYANMAR INDIA
KAZAKHSTAN NORTH KOREA KYRGYZSTAN LAOS MONGOLIA
NEPAL PAKISTAN RUSSIA TAJIKISTAN VIETNAM

How is China's government structured?
At the top of the Communist Party of China is the Central Committee; when it is not in session, the Political Bureau and its Standing Committee exercise the power of the Central Committee. The president is the official head of the state, and appoints the premier, vice premiers, state councilors, ministers of various ministries and state commissions, the auditor-general, and the secretary-general of the State Council. The National People's Congress is the country's legislative body. Members are elected only indirectly, by People's Congresses at lower levels.

What is the official title of China's current leader, Xi Jinping?
Xi is the General Secretary of the Communist Party of China, the President of the People's Republic of China, and the chairman of the Central Military Commission.

What does the design of the Chinese flag symbolize?
The flag of China is red, representing the Communist revolution. There are four small, yellow stars forming an arc around a large, yellow star. The large star represents the Communist Party, and the smaller stars represent China's four social classes (as described by Mao Zedong): peasants, workers, urban petite bourgeoisie, and national capitalists.

What is the controversy over Tibet?

In 1950 China invaded Tibet and seized control—claiming that Tibet had always been a part of China. The Dalai Lama, Tibet's spiritual and political leader, was forced into exile, where he remains a living symbol of the hope for Tibetan independence. In spite of ongoing international pressure, China has refused to relinquish control.

Is Taiwan part of China?

The Chinese say it is, but Taiwan exists in a kind of political limbo—independent from China in practice, yet unable to declare its independence, for fear that China will then seize it by force. The island was ruled by foreign powers in the 19th and 20th centuries—until the Nationalists fled there and took over in 1945.

What is China's largest city?

Shanghai is China's largest city, with a 2014 population estimate of 24 million—one of the largest cities in the world. Beijing, the capital, has a population of 19 million.

What is the main religion in China?

Though the Communist Party is officially secular, there are a number of popular religions in China. Roughly 30 percent of the population identifies as religious. The government recognizes Buddhism, Islam, Taoism, Protestantism, and Catholicism, and legally protects the followers of those faiths.

THE CIVIL WAR DECADES

HOW CHIANG KAI-SHEK SET THE STAGE FOR MAO ZEDONG

China has one of the longest and richest histories in the world, dating back almost 5,000 years. The last dynasty to rule China, the Qing, reigned from 1644 until 1912, and for the majority of this time the country enjoyed almost unparalleled prosperity. The centralized imperial government had established a thriving agriculture, and secured a high quality of living for its citizens. Toward the end of the 19th century, however, China started facing a number of internal and external problems that undermined this good fortune.

THE ENDLESS WARS

China's self-reliance under the Qing Dynasty created a strong national identity—something future leaders would try desperately

---

Right: Chiang Kai-shek in full military uniform, circa 1940.

to recreate. This solidarity fractured under the weight of roughly 75 years of almost endless war. By the mid 1850s, China had already fought—and lost—two wars with the British Empire over Britain's illegal opium trade. At the end of the first Opium War in 1842, Britain annexed Hong Kong—a significant incursion into the formerly closed off China. The French joined forces with the British for the second Opium War and, together, the Western countries easily secured the Treaties of Tianijn, also known as the "unequal treaties." As the epithet suggests, the Qing dynasty conceded heavily to the Western nations, both politically and psychologically. China was left with no option but to allow the legal trade of opium, and required to open up more ports and trade routes with Britain, France, Russia, and the United States.

Further turmoil came to China along the trade routes, and the Taiping Rebellion claimed the lives of an estimated 20,000,000 people by the time it ended in 1864. This internal con- flict marked an intensely dark chapter in Chinese history. One of the tangential effects of the Tianjin Treaties was a greater presence of Westerners in China, who brought with them something previously unheard of—Christianity.

Japanese soldiers celebrate the capture of Nanking, China. December 13-31, 1937.

Fueled by religious fervor, the followers of Hong Xiuquan (who, incidentally, believed himself to be the younger brother of Jesus Christ) sought to overthrow the empire and claim China for themselves. The Rebellion lasted 15 years, and drenched the entire southern part of the country in blood. The stability that had been the hallmark of the past 300 years was completely gone.

Already severely weakened by fighting the Opium Wars and the Taiping Rebellion, the Qing Dynasty's grasp on the country almost disappeared, in 1894, when China went to war with Japan over Korea. Like the Opium Wars, there were two iterations of the Sino-Japanese War. The first lasted just one year, from 1894 to 1895, but it set the backdrop for an intensely hostile relationship between China and Japan. When China called for peace, the result further weakened China's standing in the international community.

CHIANG KAI-SHEK'S RISE

After many years of painful deterioration, the Qing Dynasty was finally ousted by the 1911 revolution. Sun Yat-Sen was elected interim president of the Republic of China—the new name for the former empire—in 1912. Although the formation of the republic led, ultimately, to the revolution in 1949, its first result was an era of warlord rule. Though the Qing dynasty had certainly seen times of turmoil, it had also provided a unifying power center for one of the world's largest countries. Absent that harmony and solidarity, warlords began ravaging the countryside and claiming small pockets of China for themselves.

A military commander, Chiang Kai-Shek fought alongside Sun Yat-Sen in overthrowing the Qing, becoming the leader of the Chinese Nationalist Party after Sun's death in 1925. Chiang's role in unifying the country was no small feat, and fighting to regain control of the land that had been seized by the warlords

DID YOU KNOW

Despite official censorship, China has a vibrant literary tradition, including two recent Nobel literature laureates: Gao Xingjian (2000) and Mo Yan (2012). Human rights activist Liu Xiaobo won the Nobel Peace Prize in 2010.

proved extremely complicated. His methods for unifying the country were harsh at best, criminal at worst. In two short years, from 1926 to 1928, he managed to reclaim power from the warlords and establish himself as the country's sole leader. Not without paying a hefty price, however: this sudden success cost Chiang a considerable share of popular support, including that of a small group of Communists, Mao Zedong among them. Like Mao would do years later, Chiang attempted to unite the country not only under his military might, but also through an ideological campaign. The New Life Movement was Chiang's vision for a moral continuity that would bring the various factions (the still-unsettled warlords, the Communists, and his own Nationalist party) together under one identity. The New Life Movement was, really, just a reinvigoration of Confucianism, the philosophy that had been dominant across the country during the dynastic ages. In 1931, only six years after he became the leader of China, Chiang faced the first invasion by the Japanese. Another six years after that, the Japanese attempted a full-scale invasion.

During this time, the Communist party in China had grown increasingly vocal and powerful. Nationalists and Communists agreed to an uneasy truce in the face of the Japanese onslaught. "Once hostilities were forced on us in 1937," Chiang wrote, "…we did not hesitate to adopt the 'scorched-earth policy,' to 'fall back into the interior'… against the Japanese militarists in an 'absolute war.'" In 1938, Chiang destroyed the Chinese-built dikes of the Yellow River to halt the Japanese army. The move was ultimately unsuccessful. Widespread devastation ensued as the river was loosed from its constraints. Beijing fell to the Japanese, and

Right: "China Carries On." Poster by United China Relief, member agency of the National War Fund, circa 1942-44.

cosmopolitan Shanghai was pulverized by bombing raids. The Japanese occupation of the Chinese city of Nanking has a special, hellish distinction as one of the worst atrocities of the ages. This was the "Rape of Nanking," where Japanese troops launched a frenzy of civilian massacres, raped on a mass scale, and released an onslaught of stunning brutality that claimed the lives of no less than 300,000 Chinese.

The advent of Communist rule in China fueled the Cold War hysteria rampant in the United States.

The Sino-Japanese War dovetailed into World War II, when China entered the war officially after the Japanese bombing of Pearl Harbor in 1941. By 1945, 20 million Chinese citizens had been killed, and, just as the end of WWII was marked by the Russian invasion of Japan and the dropping of the atomic bomb on Hiroshima and the rest of the world readied for peacetime, the Communist-Nationalist tensions inside China rose again. To a certain extent, it was the many years of instability and hardship that the Chinese people suffered that made Mao's rise to power possible. The country was desperate for a leader who could unify, and Mao was at the right place at the right time.

MAO COMES TO POWER

Mao Zedong was the Communists' brilliant and brutal theorist and organizer. The Chinese population, by 1945, had enough of the Nationalists. In 1947, Nationalist troops began surrendering to Communist forces. Desertion continued. In early 1949, Beijing fell to the Communists. The Nationalist forces essentially melted away. Mao proclaimed the People's Republic of China on October 1, 1949. The conflict, while almost finished, was not entirely over. Chiang and 2 million Nationalists retreated to the island of Taiwan, which had been held by the Japanese from 1895 to 1945. There, Chiang established himself at the helm of the anti-Communist Republic of China.

The advent of Communist rule in China fueled the Cold War hysteria rampant in the United States. "Who lost China?" became an accusatory cry—as if China was America's to "lose." It was tiny Taiwan—Chiang Kai-shek's China, and not the colossus that was the People's Republic—that the United States held up as an antidote to the worldwide "Red contagion." Chiang Kai-shek and Taiwan took its place in the UN, and President Richard Nixon made his historic visit to Mao Zedong in 1972. It was not until Jimmy Carter's administration that the United States formally opened full diplomatic relations with the People's Republic, 30 years after its establishment. Chiang

THE DERUNG

The Derung are an ethnic group in China numbering less than 10,000. Living in the Yunnan Province, the Derung's mode of living has been traditional hunting and farming. After the advent of Communist rule, the Derung were taught Chinese. Derung girls get their faces tattooed when they are 13, with patterns varying according to family. This and other practices are dying out as the Derung are forced into more contact with modern China.

Statue of Chiang Kai-shek

Kai-shek and Taiwan became pivotal symbols in the Cold War, especially during the Korean War in the early 1950s—when the People's Republic came to the aid of North Korea. The Republic of China was deemed the "official" China in the United Nations, and given a permanent seat on the Security Council, to the exclusion of the People's Republic. In 1971, the People's Republic finally took its place in the UN.

The People's Republic of China has long refused to recognize the existence of the Republic of China (Taiwan) and has claimed Taiwan as an integral—non-negotiable—part. Long after the deaths of Chiang Kai-shek and Mao Zedong, the dispute continues. Taiwan has emerged as a democratic nation and prosperous economic power, and the People's Republic is now an economic powerhouse that dominates a huge portion of world trade.

THE CONFLICTED CHAIRMAN

MAO'S MULTIFACETED LEGACY

"THE forests are a red blooming in the frost sky," Mao Zedong wrote in a poem in 1931, at the height of his battles with Nationalists. "The anger of our good soldiers climbs through the clouds … Our huge army pours into Kiangsi / Wind and smoke whirl whirl through half the world. / We woke a million workers and peasants / to have one heart."

Mao Zedong indeed woke millions and millions of workers and peasants: the strategic organizer and polemicist led the longstanding Communist insurrection to victory over Chiang Kai-shek's Nationalists in 1949. Mao, the Great Helmsman as he was known, ruled the world's most populous nation for nearly three decades, during which the People's Republic of China made great strides. But, under Mao's harsh reign, the country also saw bloodshed, devastation, and oppression on an equally mass scale. "A revolution is not the same as inviting people to dinner or writing an essay or painting a picture or embroidering a flower,"

Paper money is a Chinese invention, which dates from the ninth century. The Chinese also get the credit—or blame—for inventing brandy and whiskey, dating back to the seventh century.

Mao wrote. "It cannot be anything so refined, so calm and gentle.... A revolution is an uprising, an act of violence whereby one class overthrows the authority of another. To put it bluntly, it was necessary to bring about a brief reign of terror in every rural area."

Before Mao's rise to power, Communism had no roots in China. The works of Karl Marx had only sporadically been translated into Chinese. The focus of the worldwide Communist movement was dismantling predatory capitalism and industrial oppression—a fundamentally Western phenomenon. China, overwhelmingly rural and agrarian, was theoretically irrelevant to Western Marxists.

China's corrupt Qing Dynasty was ousted, making way for the establishment of a republic in 1912. With it came currents of intellectual freedom and curiosity that began to permeate the country. And then, another political transformation took place in 1917, when Russia overthrew the Romanov Dynasty and, for the first time, a Communist Party took office. It was through Moscow (specifically, the Comintern, the Soviet organization tasked with fermenting the ground of worldwide revolution) that the foundations for a Chinese Communist Party were laid.

The young Mao moved from rural Shaoshan first to Beijing, and then Shanghai, where he was exposed to radical ideas and new notions of intellectual freedom. In the cities, he assumed a key role in the fledgling Communist Party. A small cadre of Marxists grew, claiming an increasingly important role in the opposition to Chiang Kai-shek and his authoritarian Nationalists. Mao helped lead a band of 1,000 that, by 1934, had grown into a force of 100,000.

In October 1934, Mao and his forces—under direct attack from the Nationalists—fled into the hinterlands. Known as the Long March, this milestone was a central event in Chinese Communist iconography. Mao and his 90,000 followers traveled about

6,000 miles of very rough country, mostly on foot, in the span of a year. Despite hardships, the outcome was triumphant: Mao's Red Army—now reduced to 20,000—was a significant fighting force that inspired immense popular support. Mao paid a deeply personal price for his militancy: His sister and second wife were executed by the Nationalists and his younger brother died during the Long March. As reporter Harrison Salisbury wrote, "Wherever the Red Army went, it performed as a living object lesson. It did not prey upon the peasants. It played the role of Robin Hood. It took from the rich landlords and wealthier peasants and gave to the poor." As time went on, the Red Army also became an effective fighting force against the marauding Japanese army.

Communist troops fought and died by Mao's military theory, encapsulated in a simple rubric: "The enemy advances; we retreat. The enemy camps; we harass. The enemy tires; we attack. The enemy retreats; we pursue." The long, bloody Nationalist-Communist struggle ended in 1949, with the installation of Mao Zedong and the Communist Party at the helm of the country.

Despite hardships, the outcome was triumphant: Mao's Red Army was a significant fighting force that inspired immense popular support.

Mao's regime set about overturning an oppressive, feudal system in a land of entrenched inequality. Development on a mass scale was accomplished with a great deal of popular support, as well as a reckless disregard for human life. Extensive land reforms, women rights advances (including the ability to own land and campaigns against prostitution), crack down of opium trafficking were all implemented with astounding efficiency. But, chief amongst Mao's accomplishments was breaking the rule of exploitative landowners, seizing their land, and dividing it among the poor—even if that meant the death of about a million landlords.

At the same time, there were plenty external factors to contend with, notably China's entry into the Korean War, which ended up wounding or killing between 700,000 and 900,000 Chinese soldiers, including Mao's eldest son. In the Soviet Union, China's political and ideological archetype, the winds started shifting after the death of Joseph Stalin. The new leader, Nikita Khrushchev, openly criticized Stalin's harsh reign and let it be known that the USSR would follow a different course.

In a 1956 speech to party leaders, Mao discussed the ideological concept of "letting a hundred flowers bloom" and—in science—"letting a hundred schools of thought contend." This initiated the Hundred Flowers Campaign, in which Mao solicited honest, uninhibited criticism from party rank and file, intellectuals, and citizens. Mao's invitation was not, however, entirely disinterested. His party had too many moving parts and factions

[
Democide is a concept formulated by the late political scientist Rudolph J. Rummel: "The murder of any person or people by a government, including genocide … and mass murder." Rummel cites Mao's China, including the Great Leap Forward and Cultural Revolution's death tolls, as prime examples.
]

Mao Zedong, left, founding father of the People's Republic of China, talking with his son Mao Anqing in Xiangshan (Fragrant Hills) in Beijing, July 1949.

to make concentration of all power to one individual manageable. Mao had many opponents in the Communist Party and in the government, and his Hundred Flowers Campaign was a mechanism to expose dissent and use the masses to curb opposition.

The Hundred Flowers Campaign, however, produced a range and depth of criticism Mao wasn't prepared for, including attacks on the party's power monopoly, its harsh intolerance towards dissent and its obsession with secrecy. There were calls for a judiciary that would be independent of the Communist Party, and an end to the privileges of the upper echelons—a criticism that resonated with masses of Chinese people who were living in abject poverty. In 1957 Mao struck back with an "anti-rightist campaign," shutting close the brief period of candor he had

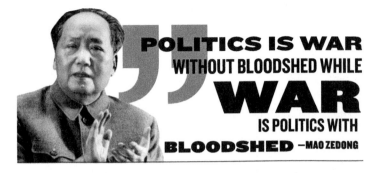

POLITICS IS WAR WITHOUT BLOODSHED WHILE WAR IS POLITICS WITH BLOODSHED —MAO ZEDONG

prompted. Without further ado, 300,000 intellectuals were designated as *rightists*—a supreme offense by the standards of the People's Republic. About half a million people were arrested.

Shortly after, Mao attempted to reinvigorate the revolutionary spark with the Great Leap Forward, a vast, ill-conceived plan to remake China's peasantry, and radically increase agricultural production through enforced collectivization of all farmland.

The Great Leap Forward wreaked deadly havoc on the Chinese people. Its effect was the opposite of what Mao intended: The grandiose plan led to a significant drop in grain production and industrial output. China was far from a land of plenty. By 1960, full-scale famine erupted. Segments of the population, facing a shortage of wheat and corn, ground elm leaves into their flour for added bulk. It is now estimated that around 42 million people died during the Great Leap Forward.

As the 1960s progressed, Mao became concerned that a weakened party bureaucracy was costing the revolution its urgency and support. Additionally, the reclusive and aging leader was the object of swirling rumors that he was dwindling and losing his grip on power. In July 1966, Mao emerged publicly in a dramatic fashion, taking a swim in the Yangtze River, to symbolize a refreshed and reinvigorated leader.

In the Cultural Revolution that followed, Mao was at the forefront, his prominence increasing to the point of worship. Nearly 5 billion badges with Mao's face were manufactured, and Mao's writing was collected in a single volume, the *Quotations from Chairman Mao Zedong*—the "Little Red Book"—that every Chinese carried.

A semi-autonomous force—the, mostly teenage, Red Guards—swung into action, smashing all "foreign" objects and whatever they regarded as counterrevolutionary. "We are the Red Guards of Chairman Mao," wrote a group of middle-school students, "and we effect the convulsions. We tear up and smash old calendars, precious vases, US and British records, superstitious lacquers and ancient paintings, and we put up the picture of Chairman Mao."

Schools across China were shut, and millions were forcibly relocated to the countryside. Scores of old-line party officials—among them Deng Xiaoping, who would lead China during the post-Mao period—were paraded through the streets in disgrace, often beaten and forced to wear dunce caps. Temples and churches were damaged; ancient artifacts destroyed as hateful vestiges of a counterrevolutionary, feudal time. Beatings, physical attacks, and murder were widespread, as was suicide. There were those who preemptively destroyed their own books and art. The zealotry and brutality spiked to horrifying heights.

Mao Zedong died in 1976, with the Cultural Revolution firmly in place. Its legacy is pervasive, and a new leadership has been forced to struggle with the damage the Cultural Revolution wrought—a touchstone that still casts a long shadow over China today.

MAO'S COMPLEX LEGACY

THE LONG AND WINDING ROAD

Mao Zedong's impact on China is deeply felt. In the 1920s, he was one of a small group of Communist activists just starting out to make themselves heard—a mere counter-balance to the ruling Nationalists.

But Mao pushed the Chinese Communists through the punishing Long March, turning them into a respected force of liberators that took on both the Japanese and the Nationalists. In 1949, he became leader of the People's Republic of China, presiding over the twists and turns of this emerging Communist power. He met with President Richard Nixon in the early 1970s, a meeting that marked a profound shift in Sino-American relationships.

Along the way, Mao became one of the century's most iconic figures. "Maoism" was widely disseminated—often in the form of the "Little Red Book"—among radical circles across the globe. In the 1960s, the Black Panthers sold copies of the "Little Red Book" as a fundraiser. Even Mao's distinctive garb, a sort of peasant-revolutionary uniform, became popular.

Nationalist rule under Chiang Kai-shek was brutal and corrupt. Mao Zedong's rule, by contrast, brought about a rise in the standard of living; he rebuilt railroads and brought inflation under control. "Raise up the landless laborer," he exhorted—and he did, paying attention to, prioritizing even, China's poorest regions. Under Communist rule, life expectancy rose dramatically. The People's Republic of China became a force to reckon with—a global power.

But these accomplishments didn't come without a human cost. The Great Leap Forward and the Cultural Revolution to a large extent happened at the expense of many lives.

China and its leaders have since defined themselves in relation to Mao Zedong's legacy—often in direct opposition. And, as an economic powerhouse, China continues to analyze, maneuver through, and shape a complicated modern history.

Communist propaganda poster, depicting citizens during Mao Zedong's rule

RELATIONS WITH RUSSIA

ALLIES, RIVALS, ENEMIES

Marxism had no roots in China before Karl Marx cited China as a prime victim of European imperialism. And, even then, China was not at all central to the Marxist worldview, nor did Marxism hold at the time any real attraction for the Chinese. The first mention of Karl Marx in a Chinese publication came in 1899; his *Communist Manifesto* was partially translated into Chinese in 1906.

In 1912 China ousted its monarchy and instituted a republic. This republic gave way to the Nationalist regime of Chiang Kai-shek, but for a while there was an openness and optimism about the possibilities of a democratic, egalitarian China. Like much of the world at that time, it had a revolutionary faction, and the Chinese were intrigued and inspirited by the Russian Revolution of 1917 and the Bolshevik seizure of power: a communist party, for the first time in history, had taken over the mechanisms of state control.

Marx spent years living and writing in London and experienced firsthand the squalor and oppression workers faced. Marxist theory was born out of industrialization, in response to the dismal conditions of the urban working class. The revolution's vanguard

Left: Nikita Khrushchev headed a delegation to Beijing, in 1959, in attendance of the 10th anniversary of the founding of the People's Republic of China.

would be the proletariat, and its locus would be the West: England, or Germany. The fact that the Communist revolution happened in Russia—with its vast rural infrastructure—was contrary to theoretical Marxism. If Russia was an unlikely candidate for a Communist revolution, China was even more so: the country was a nation of hundreds of millions of peasants.

The Chinese Communist Party received early crucial backing from the Soviet Union. Mao Zedong was a committed Marxist who fought for the elimination of capitalism. But he was not tied to a static theory; he took Marxist-Leninist thought and infused it with a strong dose of functionalism. Mao's campaigns took him to the countryside and brought him in touch with the rural classes, where he realized that the burning issue in China was not factory conditions or the extrication of surplus value, but peasant exploitation in all its manifestations. A Chinese revolution, therefore, would never originate in the urban proletariat; there simply wasn't enough of it. But Mao cared little about academic theorizing; he was a shrewd organizer and a fighter, and was set on establishing Communist rule in China.

When the People's Republic of China was established in 1949, the very fact of its existence presented a challenge to the Soviet Union. Moscow had been the undisputed worldwide seat of the revolution. Now, there were two seats (Moscow and Beijing) and a whole new doctrine (Maoism).

The Soviet Union needed an alliance with Communist China; China needed assistance from the Soviet Union. In the early years of the People's Republic, the Soviet Union provided massive amounts of aid. Yet, contrary to the nightmarish vision of American cold war fearmongers, who anticipated a united, hostile bloc of two huge Red nations, the two Communist giants found it hard to stay in lockstep.

Mao Zedong began exporting his own notions of revolution and social change, seeking to make Beijing the new capital of the Communist world. To Soviet leader Nikita Khrushchev's intense displeasure, anti-colonialist fighters throughout Africa expressed a greater affinity for Maoism than they did for the Soviet framework.

China in the 1950s was imbued with revolutionary fervor, but it also harbored serious fears for its own security. The United States directly engaged the Chinese during the Korean War, and American troops gained a permanent foothold in South Korea. Taiwan, headed by Mao's old foe Chiang Kai-shek, and backed fully by the United States, called steadily for the reinstallation of Nationalist rule in mainland China. And the Soviet Union under Khrushchev was a different place than it had been under the harsh rule of Joseph Stalin: more open and more conciliatory toward the West. Mao was committed to expanding the military might of China. He

In **1976** an increasingly infirm Mao Zedong died after nearly 30 years as leader of the People's Republic of China. Within a relatively short time, China radically changed its political and economic direction.

A WORD ABOUT

The Uighur are a sizable minority in the Chinese region of Xinjiang, a geopolitically sensitive region whose borders include Russia, Mongolia, Pakistan, Afghanistan, and India. The Uighur are Muslim, and they have a linguistic and ethnic link to Turkey and Central Asia. Among them, there has been significant ethnic unrest and a separatist movement, pointing to the fact that the People's Republic of China is not as homogenous as many in the West imagine—or the Chinese would like to portray.

Nikita Khrushchev and Mao Zedong toast each other, 1959.

was keen on the People's Republic developing atomic weapons. It was expected that the Soviet Union would provide the technical know-how and support. As time went on, Soviet reluctance to aid the Chinese in developing an atomic bomb became apparent.

There were intrinsic, longstanding conflicts between the two superpowers that shared an over-2,000-mile-long border and often vied for influence and regional dominance. A shaky alliance based on different versions of Communism could not cover up larger differences. The two leaders also felt an overt personal antagonism. In private meetings, Mao took a sharply patronizing tone with the Soviet leader.

Relations deteriorated sharply in 1960, when Khrushchev withdrew the scientific and technical support so vital to the People's Republic, scuttling any hope for a Chinese atomic bomb developed with Soviet backing. "When they say that this cannot be done, and that cannot be done, ignore them," Mao stated. "With indomitable and indefatigable effort, the Chinese people will steadily obtain their objectives." The national objective of developing a Chinese atomic bomb was accomplished in 1964 and China joined the select club of nuclear powers.

Khrushchev was ousted from power in 1964, and a new leadership coalesced around Leonid Brezhnev. It did nothing to halt deteriorating relations, which ranged from the potentially catastrophic (border clashes) to the farcical (in the 1960s, the Soviets insisted that visiting Chinese prove they had been vaccinated).

The overt hostility faded over the years, and tectonic geopolitical shifts in the 1970s changed relations. China today bears little resemblance to its Maoist past. Its nuclear capabilities have progressed, as has its ability to deliver those weapons by air and sea. China has also sent rockets into space. Mao's prediction that it could all be done without Soviet help has proven nothing but true.

UNDER THE CHINESE THUMB

SIXTY-FIVE YEARS IN TIBET

Tenzin Gyatso was born in 1935. He is better known by his title: the 14th Dalai Lama. This Dalai Lama was 16 when he assumed his position as both spiritual and political leader of Tibet. He has been in exile from Tibet since 1959 and is the living symbol of Tibetan opposition to harsh Chinese control.

Tibet declared independence from China in 1913, but Mao asserted that the mountainous country had "always" been part of China. The People's Liberation Army invaded in 1950, and in 1951 negotiations over the future of Tibetan sovereignty resulted in a framework known as the Seventeen Points. The purpose of these negotiations, to the Chinese government, was a Tibetan "return to the big family of the Motherland—the People's Republic of China." In other words, Tibet would be annexed to China. Religious freedom was to be guaranteed, reforms were to be gradual, and the Dalai Lama was to keep his authority. In reality, however, Communism and theocracy are fundamentally irreconcilable: Repressive Chinese rule resulted in a Tibetan revolt in 1959, which led to a complete Chinese takeover and the Dalai Lama's flight to India, where he has maintained a government-in-exile ever since.

In 2008 protests against Chinese rule spread, and were brutally suppressed by the Chinese authorities. The Dalai Lama

The Potala Palace in Lhasa, Tibet, once the home of the Dalai Lama, is now a museum.

may have become an internationally prominent figure, but Tibet is still part of China, more than half a century later, which raises a great deal of questions about Tibetan culture and identity and its framing in relation to China.

DENG XIAOPING & PRIVATIZATION

MOVING CHINA TOWARD INDEPENDENT COMMERCE

Communism in Eastern Europe collapsed in 1989. Within two short years, the Union of Soviet Socialist Republics was a thing of the past. The fall of the Iron Curtain led many to declare Communism dead. But the death certificate was somewhat premature. It's easy to forget that China still is, in name at least, Communist.

China is an industrial giant, outpacing nearly the entire world in production, supplying an enormous portion of what used to be provided by America's manufacturing base. Almost every American household is full of items, from clothing to appliances to packaged food, that have been made in China. News stories about China's expanding influence abound. But that economic

Right: A mural in Shenzhen commemorating Deng Xiaoping's founding of China's first Special Economic Zone.

百年不动摇

中共深圳市委
市美术广

President Ford, Vice Premier Deng Xiaoping, and Deng's interpreter have a cordial chat during an informal meeting in Beijing, in 1975.

might has also engendered social problems: pollution, corruption, crime, unemployment. China now has issues that have plagued every other industrialized society before it. This may still be the People's Republic of China; Communist rule has not been overturned. Yet the transformation is astounding.

President Richard Nixon's historic visit to China in 1972 is now a distant memory. At the time, he pierced the veil of secrecy on a vast nation still under the rule of Mao Zedong. A year after Mao's death in 1976, Deng Xiaoping emerged as "paramount leader," and pragmatism began to overtake ideology.

"Paramount leader," as vague as that might sound, was a very specific designation. Deng eschewed formal titles. This leader, who so upended the People's Republic, passed on formal recognition, preferring instead to wield vast power behind more obscure titles.

EARLY DAYS

In 1919 the 16-year-old Deng was one of 92 Chinese students who traveled abroad for a prolonged study in Paris. Also among them was Zhou Enlai, for decades the subordinate to Mao Zedong and the diplomatic face of China to the West. Deng returned home to China in the 1920s as an active, committed Communist and was an invaluable asset to Mao during the arduous Long March.

> *Deng said, "It doesn't matter whether a cat is black or white as long as it catches mice."*

He became a prominent figure in the newly established People's Republic of China, despite growing friction between Mao and himself. They clashed especially after the catastrophic Great Leap Forward, when Deng proposed that the peasantry be allowed a small measure of private farming—anathema to Maoist orthodoxy. Citing an old proverb, Deng said, "It doesn't matter whether a cat is black or white as long as it catches mice." That became a popular maxim in the years after Mao's death, as China opened up to the West. In the short run, however, Deng's pragmatism and willingness to bend the rules of Marxism cost him dearly.

Deng ran afoul of the Red Guards during the turbulent Cultural Revolution in the 1960s. His eldest son was harassed at the Beijing University campus, leading him to jump from a window. Though he survived the fall, his back was broken, leaving him paralyzed.

With Mao becoming infirm, the resourceful Deng Xiaoping rose again to prominence. The growing pains within the Chinese power structure continued. Zhou Enlai, Mao's lieutenant, died in January 1976. Long considered the humane, reformist face of the Chinese revolution, Zhou's death prompted an outpouring of public mourning. Months later, his memory was invoked as widespread calls for reform turned into nationwide demonstrations. The populist sentiment was, once again, suppressed.

LEADERSHIP BY ANY OTHER NAME

Deng's pragmatism still serves as a guiding principle. Deng introduced capitalist concepts to the People's Republic. Under his leadership, special economic zones were established that tripled the average income. He shepherded negotiations with the United Kingdom that returned the British colony of Hong Kong to Chinese rule. Deng pledged that Hong Kong's prosperous economic infrastructure would remain unchanged under Chinese sovereignty, and he delivered.

He also significantly eased the Communist Party's vast control apparatus that, until then, permeated every corner of Chinese life. The Chinese were finally allowed to study overseas. He opened China to foreign trade, technology, and investment, which allowed people to get their hands on telephones, televisions, and washing machines. Collective farms and communes were discontinued. Discos and nightclubs appeared. Newspapers began to feature glossy ads. In the original iteration of the People's Republic of China, these developments would have been unforgiveable sacrilege. In short, Deng pushed the austere, puritanical Maoist ethos out the window.

Deng died in 1997. The course he charted for China has since grown exponentially. China is today the world's biggest economy, having recently exceeded the United Stated in global trade, goods, and services.

The irony is that China under Deng began seeing capitalist and industrial excesses of the sort Marx observed in 19th-century Britain. A hasty boom of industry brings with it problems such as exploitative labor practices, the use of child labor, and unsafe factory conditions.

"To get rich," the revamped Party saying went, "is glorious." The new China, which had suffered under Mao's orthodoxy and austerity, now suffered a new brand of injustice and deprivation.

Deng did nothing to alter the authoritarian power structure of China's governing

[
After discovering the means for making silk threads into fabric, the Chinese later also invented silk screen printing, which first took place around 1,000 AD.
]

TAKEOUT TAKEOVER

In 2014 a restaurant opened in Shanghai serving a novel cuisine: fortune cookies, sweet-and-sour chicken, and General Tso's chicken. The restaurant—called, appropriately enough, Fortune Cookie—served Chinese-American food, which basically has only a passing similarity to indigenous Chinese cooking and is an unknown commodity in China itself. The restaurant's clientele is a mixture of curious locals and American expatriates.

party and Tibet was never granted independence. In fact, Chinese control has steadily tightened. An influx of Chinese living in Tibet poses a real challenge to indigenous Tibetan culture.

Amid controversy, China's economic role and political prominence have continued to expand. Beijing was the site of the 2008 Summer Olympics: a prize slot for a country that had, decades past, been an isolated, poverty-striken giant. The headlines coming out of the country are now familiar: dissidents suppressed; restrictions on artistic freedom and freedom of expression; a judicial system with a conviction rate of 99 percent; worker safety issues; crime; air pollution and the destruction of the environment; fluctuations of Chinese currency, stocks, and trading.

"When China wakes," Napoleon is alleged to have claimed, "it will shake the world." Finally, China *has* awakened, and the balance of world power is shifting.

THE FOUR MODERNIZATIONS

EXPANSION AND REPRESSION IN THE AGE OF DENG XIAOPING

The Four Modernizations were a crucial ideological construct during the post-Mao era. Gone were the exhortations for class struggle and Communism on its global march. China's priority became to modernize agriculture, industry, defense, and technology. The People's Republic of China was easing some of the ideological constraints that had been in place for decades. The turbulence and chaos of the Cultural Revolution were still on the minds of Chinese policymakers; they wanted a calmer, more productive kind of revolution.

Deng used the Four Modernizations to steer China on its new, capitalist-friendly course. "Our fundamental task must be to

Above: A farmer carries rice seedlings for transplant into a water-filled paddy in Mingshi, Guangxi Province.

develop the productive forces, shake off poverty, build a strong, prosperous country, and improve the living conditions of the people," he declared.

Richard Nixon helped initiate the process of normalizing Sino-American relations. President Jimmy Carter extended an official recognition of the People's Republic of China in 1979 and established formal diplomatic relations that viewed Beijing as the sole legitimate government of the Chinese people (leaving Taiwan in diplomatic limbo). "We renounce class struggle as the central focus," Deng said in a speech in 1978, "and instead take up economic development as our central focus." A business-friendly climate was emerging in China.

The Chinese government deemed this economic course "market socialism," a somewhat contradictory term. It suggested that, although China might abandon the entrenched Marxist-Leninist class struggle mantra, the central tenets of the revolution would not be discarded. The lineage—Marx to Lenin to Mao—would be retained.

As laudable as the Four Modernizations were, there was also a glaring lag when it came to human rights. In a 1978 essay, the dissident Wei Jingsheng publicly called for a Fifth Modernization: democracy. "Can the Four Modernizations be achieved in a society governed by overlords and worked by professional and amateur slaves?" Wei asked. "Impossible! The situation in our country presents a tragic reality: Not long ago we were even forbidden to mention the Four Modernizations. The fact that we can talk about them now is put forward as a great dispensation, a favor granted us by those on high. Aren't you overwhelmed with gratitude?" This candor earned Wei a nearly two-decade stay in prison.

THE TOP 10

MOST INFLUENTIAL CHINESE FILM DIRECTORS

1 Ang Lee *The Wedding Banquet* (1993) brought the director great acclaim; his *Crouching Tiger, Hidden Dragon* (star Michelle Yeoh, pictured right) won the Oscar for Best Foreign Language Film of 2000. Lee has won the Best Director Oscar twice, for *Brokeback Mountain* (2005) and *Life of Pi* (2012).

2 Ann Hui Her work reflects the Hong Kong New Wave and highlights a wide range of social concerns. *The Postmodern Life of My Aunt* (2006) concerns an elderly retiree who is cheated out of her savings.

3 Lou Ye A cursory look at Lou Ye's cinematic themes shows just how far China has changed in the past few decades. *Summer Palace* (2006) depicts a free-spirited female Beijing University student and the subsequent trauma of Tiananmen Square. The protagonist of *Spring Fever* (2009) is a gay travel agent. Lou Ye is also associated with the French film scene.

4 **John Woo** If film violence is an art form, Woo (pictured above, with Nicolas Cage in *Windtalkers*) is its Picasso. American audiences became aware of Woo through mainstream films like *Face/Off* (1997) with John Travolta and Nicolas Cage, but real aficionados know to look to Woo's rawer, fascinatingly intricate pre-Hollywood efforts, including *A Better Tomorrow* (1986), *The Killer* (1989), and *Hard Boiled* (1992).

5 **Tian Zhuangzhuang** Much of Tian Zhuangzhuang's work reflects a strong interest in minority communities: *On the Hunting Ground* (1985) is set in Mongolia, and Tibet is the scene of *The Horse Thief* (1986). His directorial efforts tackling the impact of the Great Leap Forward and the Cultural Revolution earned him governmental censure that sidelined his career for a time.

6 Zhang Yimou A seminal contributor to Chinese film's Fifth Generation—the post-Cultural Revolution generation—Zhang Yimou first became familiar to American moviegoers with 1991's *Raise the Red Lantern*.

7 Chen Kaige Another Fifth Generation film-maker, his *Farewell My Concubine* (1993) garnered acclaim in the United States. His work has touched on deli-cate political themes in efforts such as *Yellow Earth* (1984) and 2002's *Together with You*.

8 Tsui Hark His blend of classic Chinese narrative, kung fu, and special effects constitute the *wuxia* genre. *Peking Opera Blues* (1986) is one of his standouts, along with *Once Upon a Time in China* (1991), *The Blade* (1995), and *Seven Swords* (2005).

9 Wong Kar-wai He won Best Director at the 1997 Cannes Film Festival, becoming the first Chinese director to do so. He uses visual metaphor and symbolism in films such as 1994's *Chungking Express, In the Mood for Love* (2000), and the science fiction-themed *2046* (2004).

10 Feng Xiaogang This director's films are more mainstream than those of his more political and social-minded colleagues, although his earlier films earned him his share of official displea-sure because of their politics. His films, including *Cell Phone* (2003) and *If You Are the One* (2008), have been enormously successful.

THE EIGHT ELDERS

WHO RULES CHINA?

Like Mao's, Deng Xiaoping's leadership was not always undisputed. Deng experienced the extreme twists and turns of Chinese politics, and took great care to associate himself with reliable allies.

The Eight Elders were eight Party members—Deng among them—who ran China, hidden from the light of public scrutiny. It was a shadow government within an already very opaque power construct.

Right: Deng Xiaoping and his wife are briefed by Johnson Space Center director Dr. Christopher C. Kraft. They received a complete review of NASA's manned space program using scale models and flight simulators.

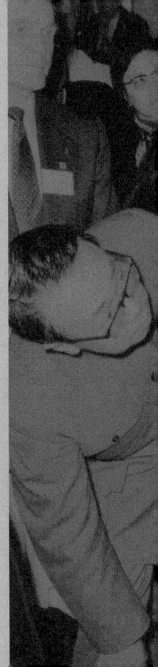

1989

THE YEAR COMMUNISM FELL

THE death of Mao Zedong in 1976 signaled a momentous change in the direction of the People's Republic of China. Similar events were happening in the Soviet Union, where the passing of the old guard also represented a fundamental shift. Mikhail Gorbachev assumed the helm of the USSR in 1985. He was the first Soviet leader born after the Communist revolution of 1917, and too young to have fought or commanded troops during World War II. Like Deng Xiaoping, Gorbachev wanted to do away with old political methods and dogmatism. The Soviet system was sluggish and inefficient, and it could not provide for the needs of its citizens. It was secretive and dictatorial, increasingly out of sync with the rest of the world.

Europe in the 1980s aligned itself according to what the battlefield had looked like at the end of World War II in 1945. The Soviet army had occupied most of Eastern Europe, so those nations were reconstituted as quasi-autonomous Communist states answering to Moscow. Rebellions had become an endemic

Right: A mass demonstration on China's National Day outside the Gate of Heavenly Peace, Tiananmen, during the Cultural Revolution of the late 1960s.

phenomenon. A mass uprising in Hungary in 1956 was violently suppressed. A decade later, Alexander Dubcek, a reformist and liberal Communist, took power for a brief interval in Czechoslovakia—known as the Prague Spring—and was quickly toppled by Soviet power in 1968. In Poland in the late 1970s, the Solidarity labor movement under Lech Walesa also attempted to loosen the strictures of Soviet control, only to fall under the imposition of martial law.

> *The army called out its tanks, and the troops fired into the crowd of unarmed protestors, most of them students.*

Gorbachev quickly eased the more repressive aspects of Soviet control. He did so faster and more thoroughly than anyone would have thought possible. His message was received loud and clear in Eastern Europe, as popular sentiment for true independence swept throughout the Soviet satellite countries.

In the past, the Soviet Union had not shied away from suppressing dissent with brute force. In 1989, however, Mikhail Gorbachev did something unprecedented: he refrained from meddling in the political movements in Eastern Europe, thus dismantling his own empire. Poland, Hungary, Czechoslovakia, Bulgaria, and Romania all broke off from Soviet control. East Germany dissolved. Latvia, Estonia, and Lithuania—the Baltic states—claimed hard-won independence. Romania's changes involved bloodshed; its longtime strongman, Nicolae Ceausescu, was executed. The road ahead for these countries was not easy. But something of vast historical importance had taken place: Within two years, the Soviet Union was no more.

All this was very much on the minds both of the Chinese government and the Chinese people. Deng Xiaoping was already loosening his grip on the Chinese, and had become internationally prominent (Deng was *Time* magazine's Man of the Year twice—a rarity). But his authoritarian tendencies ran deep and the new political direction from Moscow was cause for alarm. The Soviet Union was legislating itself out of existence. The Chinese people, meanwhile, took their government's proclamations of new political freedom seriously.

The death of the liberal-minded Communist Party Secretary Hu Yaobang on April 15, 1989, sparked a series of demonstrations in Beijing's half-mile-long Tiananmen Square in favor of greater reforms. Within a week, the protestors were numbering 100,000. In May 3,000 students camping the square began a hunger strike, eliciting widespread sympathy. By May 19, the streets of Beijing were choked with a million people marching to demonstrate their solidarity with the hunger strikers. On May 20, martial law was imposed in parts of Beijing. Despite popular support, the Chinese leadership, unlike the Soviets, wasn't having any of it.

Gorbachev came to Beijing in May, seeking to repair long-frayed relations between the Soviet Union and the People's Republic. This was highly auspicious, as no Soviet leader had visited Beijing since the days of Khrushchev. Protestors and democracy advocates welcomed Gorbachev as an inspirational figure who was considered sympathetic to the people's concerns. For Deng Xiaoping, however, the Gorbachev visit turned into a veritable disaster. The international press had been invited to

Beijing to spread the good news of Chinese-Soviet reconciliation. The prime story, instead, became the news of a mass uprising.

Hunger strike was an effective, nonviolent mode of militancy. But as a way of soliciting sympathy from the Beijing authorities, it failed pathetically. On June 3, according to eyewitness accounts, "three thousand soldiers and armed police with helmets and clubs… surrounded the civilians…Ten minutes later, they threw 20 tear-gas bombs. While everyone was blinded by the gas, the soldiers wielded clubs, and old people and children fell to the ground." The agitated crowd grew increasingly vociferous and more troops eventually arrived, firing their guns. In the middle of the night, "a red signal flare ripped the night sky…. Students found that they were surrounded by armed soldiers…."

The next day, troops occupied the square. The demonstrators were suppressed with shocking brutality. The army called out its tanks, and the troops fired into the crowd of unarmed protestors, most of them students. The death toll was estimated at 400 to 800; the injured numbered in the thousands. In one of the most iconic images of the last century, an unidentified student boldly stands in the tanks' pathway, blocking their advance.

The armed soldiers beat and shot at the demonstrators in full view of a horrified world. The death toll was substantial. The Chinese government continued its retaliation by executing democratic activists in Beijing, Shanghai, and other cities around the country. Repression, supposedly a relic from an era bygone, had been revived.

The world was shocked, marking the events as a brutal response from a leadership set on maintaining total control at any cost. But Tiananmen Square was viewed differently inside China. After so many years of swift and unforgiving hostility to dissent, Deng Xiaoping's handling of the protesters was actually seen by many as a moderate reaction. The international response, however, failed to take the context of Deng's actions into account.

Deng and his faction kept their power, but his image abroad as the inspired architect of a new China was injured. The Chinese government felt increasingly threatened by displays of public assertiveness and calls for democratization. And it felt particularly threatened as the political ground was shifting radically: By 1991, the Eastern European Communist bloc and the USSR were gone.

At the beginning of 1992, the almost 90-year-old Deng embarked on a one-month trip across southern China—the Southern Tour, as it was known—that took him to the epicenter of his new, capitalist-friendly creation. For Deng, it was a bold, dramatic gesture. His intention was to polish his tarnished image and permanently implant his vision of market socialism into China's political fabric; it was Deng's swan song. He had succeeded: China's road to capitalist expansion was finally unimpeded.

A NEW NATIONALISM

FINDING A MODERN IDENTITY

The People's Republic of China was forged with determination, sacrifice, and suffering—as almost all new national identities are. Historically, China had been a vast land of overlapping influences, presided over by a centralized government, with diverse regions and cultures. Spheres of the country

had been occupied by European powers who had no qualms about exercising brute force to impose their will. After the fall of the Qing Dynasty and the foundation of a republic in 1912, large swathes of the country remained in the hands of powerful regional warlords.

Mao and the Communist Party bulldozed their way into creating a more cohesive, unified China. That brought her away from the mercy of European imperialism, and the Chinese people were finally no longer subject to the whims of mercurial warlords. The price was high: the convulsions of the Great Leap Forward and the Cultural Revolution, famine, and political repression on a grand scale.

As China discarded its Communist strictures, the country was flooded with both the desire for change and the wish to

resurrect old modes of living that had been banned for decades by the Communist government. Some of the tectonic changes included the introduction of Western lifestyles—shopping at the mall, owning a car, capitalizing on investments. In post-Maoist China, the fact that the masses could now listen to pop music, make money, and travel was transformative. In less than a decade after Deng opened the doors of China to the world, more than 50 million Chinese began learning English. They ate fast food and rode Japanese bicycles. Overseas Chinese students—once an anomaly—became commonplace at colleges and universities. The decades-long volatility between the People's Republic and Taiwan also began to ease. Taiwan slowly morphed into a democratic, prosperous island nation and abandoned the claim that it represented all of China. The overheated rhetoric eased, and the Cold War tensions dissipated as the Cold War ended. The People's Republic absorbed hyper-capitalist Hong Kong. Beijing was now much more interested in making a profit than an ideological statement. The world took note.

Those astonishing changes have been both for the better and for the worse. The newfound freedoms produced new problems, which isn't so unusual. Post-Communist Russia affords its citizens liberties that would have been unthinkable during the eras of Stalin, Khrushchev, and Brezhnev. But a measure of freedom for some means a measure of freedom for all: the proletariat, and the Russian Mafia alike.

The Chinese economic boom, the *New York Times* reported, "has created opportunities for women" and "has also fostered a resurgence of long-repressed traditional values." The Communist Party prided itself on its egalitarian, antisexist policies, and its strides were held up all over Asia as an example. But now, "More and more men and women say a woman's place is in the home, as wealthy men take mistresses in a contemporary reprise of the concubine system, and as pressure for women to marry young remains intense. In the office, Socialist-era egalitarianism has been replaced by open sexism, in some cases reinforced by the law."

It is not uncommon for social forces long suppressed to resurface when given the chance. The officially atheistic People's Republic banned religion and disavowed the ancient teachings of Confucius—a suppression that increased with violent force during the Cultural Revolution, when temples and religious shrines were destroyed. In this climate of greater tolerance, the long-suppressed tenets of Confucianism and those of Buddhism and Taoism have experienced a resurgence.

Religion and time-honored cultural mores are also on the rise for reasons unrelated to political oppression. China's unparalleled economic boom caused massive population movements, as a

[
One of the most recognizable landmarks in the world, the Great Wall of China was constructed during the Ming dynasty (1368-1644) and stretches 5,500 miles.
]

MY NAME IS...

The spelling of Chinese names has long presented problems for Westerners. The standard system of transliteration was known as Wade-Giles, which was ultimately deemed inaccurate. It was replaced by the more accurate Pinyin system. Thus, China's capital— rendered Peking in Wade-Giles—has been restyled in the Pinyin system as Beijing. Mao Zedong had been formerly referred to in the West as Mao Tse-tung.

The ancient pagodas of the Forbidden City are surrounded by the modern buildings of Beijing.

money-making ethos swept into the society at large. Entire villages have given way to high-rises and industrial sprawl. In the decades to come, China will undergo the largest human migration in global history, as some 250 million rural residents relocate to urban areas. Village traditions, passed down from generation to generation, are hard to maintain in crowded cities.

Some of the dislocation is the result of issues specific to China. Old city streets, for instance, were constructed to let rickshaws pass; modernizing the streets for cars and buses is a challenge. Yet, as more of traditional China gives way, the desire to preserve something of the past becomes greater.

China has become a very complicated place, presenting complex issues for the Chinese government and the people alike. It has come a long way from the old, traditional China. The Marxist-Leninist model has dissipated, replaced with market capitalism. The Chinese authorities perpetually oscillate between the need for openness and an instinct toward authoritarianism. In 1989, there was no ambiguity when peaceful protests were put down with a vengeance. As China continues to emerge, it faces challenges and pressure to improve the extent of its reach. "The Soviet Union's today is China's tomorrow" was a saying of Mao Zedong. Today, that prediction seems quite prescient.

EMPTY BIRD'S NEST SYNDROME

IF YOU BUILD IT, THEY WILL COME. THEN, WHAT?

Beijing was the host city of the 2008 Summer Olympics. It was a critical moment for the Chinese government, undeniable proof that the country had indeed arrived on the world stage. One of the standouts of the event was the massive, futuristic-looking National Stadium, with its arresting latticework shell, quickly dubbed the Bird's Nest. Construction costs

ran to about $500 million for a huge stadium that seats 90,000 people. But when the Olympics ended, Beijing was suddenly faced with the looming possibility that the Bird's Nest might turn out to be a white elephant.

This is often the fate of imposing Olympic structures. After the games end, there isn't much use for them. The post-Olympics use for the Bird's Nest has yet to be found. Beijing's soccer team declined its use; in essence, it has become a tourist destination, but one unable to generate any significant revenue.

To complicate matters further, dissident artist Ai Weiwei, who had helped with the design of the Bird's Nest, publicly disavowed his efforts on the eve of the Olympics. "Almost 60 years after the founding of the People's Republic," he announced in a statement, "we still live under autocratic rule.... We do not have an open media even though freedom of expression is more valuable than life itself."

AI'S ART

HOW CAN ARTISTIC EXPRESSION FLOURISH WHEN THE ARTIST IS CONTROLLED?

China's suppression can be concisely summarized: "We have a government that, after 60 years in power, doesn't give its own people the right to choose its leaders."

That short, frank statement comes from Ai Weiwei, the prominent Chinese artist, free-speech advocate, and human rights activist. His father, renowned poet Ai Qing, was exiled to a labor camp during the Cultural Revolution. Ai Weiwei gave the Chinese authorities a black eye during the 2008 Summer Olympics. After serving as one of the designers of the striking National Stadium—the Bird's Nest—he publicly denounced his efforts as incompatible with the general culture of repression and corruption endemic in the Chinese government.

Left: Ai Weiwei's "Trace" installation at the "@Large: Ai Weiwei on Alcatraz" exhibit on the Alcatraz Prison, in the San Francisco bay, California.

Above: An employee poses next to gold-plated "Zodiac Heads" by Chinese artist Ai Weiwei during a photocall in central London. Right: Ai Weiwei poses in the middle of his work made of 100 tree parts, titled "Rooted Upon" (2009) at the *Haus der Kunst* (House of Art) during the presentation of his exhibition "So Sorry."

His art is innovative and deeply political. In 2010, he presented at London's Tate Modern a startling installation of 100 million porcelain sunflower seed husks. The sheer scale of "Sunflower Seeds" was a comment on China's outsized role in the global economy; the porcelain is part of traditional Chinese craft-making.

Ai Weiwei has been beaten and detained. He is under regular official surveillance, and—as of this writing—unable to leave China. In 2015 Amnesty International bestowed upon him their top honor, the Ambassador of Conscience Award. "I think as an artist," Ai said, "I use my own way to fulfill my responsibility to society. Whether we have compassion for our own people or other countries, we all have to take responsibility."

CONTROLLED SENTENCES

CHINA, THE MEDIA, AND THE FIGHT FOR FREE EXPRESSION

I n the past few decades, China has opened up in spectacular ways. But "opening up" is a relative term. China, for all its massive shifts, is still a one-party state with severe limits on free expression. Its jails hold dissidents; its art and writing remain under governmental control.

But the outside world has been difficult for the authorities of the People's Republic to block out. Since the 1970s, Chinese viewers have been able to tune in to lively, unfettered entertainment on Hong Kong TV.

Additionally, the emergence of the Web as a major media force has presented authorities with new censorship challenges. It is one thing to tightly control print media; it is quite another to clamp down on the porous Internet. More than 600 million Chinese people are online; 300 million are blogging. In response, the government implemented easily monitored gateways to filter out unwelcome information or forbidden opinions. According to Liu Xiaobo, the long-imprisoned Chinese writer and dissident, and

給「十八大」的十八大
② 尊重網絡自由，
G○○gle 停止封鎖網頁
✗ You✗ube

A pro-democracy activist holds a placard symbolising the internet restrictions in mainland China during a protest in front of the Chinese liaison office against Beijing's central government in Hong Kong, November 8, 2012.

recipient of the Nobel Peace Prize in 2010, the government's censorship and surveillance program even had its own name, "The Golden Shield," but was sardonically dubbed "The Great Firewall of China." There also is a massive, thousands-strong Web-policing force, warning users that they've gone too far, or shutting down operations altogether. The aim is to create, in essence, a curated online system to conform to the views of the Communist Party. Satire is usually a byproduct of repression. Chinese Internet users dubbed this pervasive authoritarian control "being harmonized."

Liu Xiaobo has regarded the Internet as the foundation of free expression. "The Communist regime," he wrote, "always obsessed with media control, has been frantic to keep up with Chinese Web users. It tries this, it tries that, fidgeting and twitching through a range of ludicrous policy contortions in its attempts to stay on top of things."

The Internet provides a platform for signature-gathering, open letters, basic information exchange: everything can be implemented from a home computer and disseminated internationally. The Internet is, also, an efficient way to spread ideas that conform to the official view.

With freedom of assembly hardly guaranteed for Chinese citizens, the Web functions as a virtual town hall or protest meeting. "China," Liu observed ruefully, "has a rich tradition of persecuting people for their words." This has not stopped, but it has at least been combatted.

Recently, China blocked foreign Internet sites that list embarrassing disclosures of the Chinese leadership's profitable offshore holdings. The government obstructed access to search-engine terms relevant to the carnage at Tiananmen Square as well. On June 4—the anniversary of the 1989 violence—many Chinese sites go down for "maintenance." On June 4, 2012, Chinese stocks fell some 64 points. "Six-four" is the abbreviation for June 4; the government sought to block all mentions of "six" and "four" in combination, and the stock news was therefore censored. Online discussions about the 2011 wave of democratic protests that swept the Middle East were also blocked, with authorities on the hunt for words such as "Tunisia" and "Egypt."

The censorship can be erratic. Foreign films and television shows—viewed online—are given a greater degree of latitude. The Netflix series *House of Cards*, about the byzantine power structure of Washington, in which China plays a part, enjoys an avid Chinese fan base, including Chinese leadership.

THE NEXT SUPERPOWER?

CHINA AS A GLOBAL FORCE

IS China already a superpower? Or is it the next superpower? How does it rate against the United States? "Superpower" is a notoriously difficult term to peg down. For four decades after World War II, the world was more or less neatly divided into two superpowers: the United States and the Soviet Union. The Soviet implosion, however, in 1989, left the United States as the only true global superpower.

But, does the U.S. still hold the monopoly on global power and influence? Its influence is certainly on the decline, and China is on an astonishing economic trajectory, surpassing the United States as the world's biggest economy.

And, even if threats to China's sovereignty are fictional rather than real, China has been flexing its muscles on the army front as well, steadily increasing its military presence in the Pacific Rim.

Even so, it remains hard to separate honest evaluations of China's power and influence from age-old, stereotypical narratives that cast China as a nation of more than a billion people on a determined march. Although challenged by political commentators for its credibility, a 2015 article in the *New York Post* purported to have the details of decades-long Chinese subversion in the United States, part of a top-secret undertaking to have China attain global supremacy in 2049, the 100th anniversary of Communist rule.

The second half of the 20th century was dominated by the superpower concept, but it remains an open question whether the superpower motif will dominate this century. Perhaps it is a concept that has run its course, a vestige of Cold War-era geopolitics. And then there's also the question that both the United States and China will have to answer: Is being a superpower even desirable? The United States and China are both struggling—to varying extrents—with an economically disadvantaged underclass and an infrastructure in desperate need of updating. The price tag for attaining superpower status is astronomical. And there's no better reminder in recent history, than the Soviet Union.

MADE IN CHINA

THE MANUFACTURING OF AN ECONOMIC POWERHOUSE

"IN the southeastern city of Wenzhou," journalist Duncan Hewitt wrote, "Mr. Song was growing tired of his old car. He'd had it for a few years and now… he felt it was time for something a little more stylish. After some careful research he found just the model he was looking for, a popular French car, now being manufactured in central China. He wasn't too happy about the price quoted by his local dealer… so he got online, and soon found a website devoted to this particular model."

In and of itself, there is nothing interesting about this story; it describes the way a huge part of the world goes about its

Above: Chinese workers in a cast iron foundry.

business. But in the People's Republic of China, this little story epitomizes the vast changes the country has undergone, including the presence of capitalist car dealerships, and the fact that French cars can be purchased in China—and researched online. China's development is one of the most exemplary cases in modern history.

Until recently, China had been a closed country, still in thrall to the teachings of Mao Zedong. By 2014, Chinese exports had risen to some $2.3 trillion. Electronic equipment represented the lion's share of exports, at 24.4 percent. Machines, engines, and pumps came in second, at 17 percent; and third on the list was furniture, lighting, and signs, at 4 percent. One of the most distinctive things about China's growth is the sheer scale of everything.

Europe and the United States have already experienced industrialization and its attendant (and still lingering) effects: exploitation, poverty, the destruction of natural resources. China is going through a similarly concentrated, hyper-rapid industrialization.

And yet, even with a soaring economy, millions of Chinese citizens struggle for access to fundamental needs, like blankets for the winter and clean drinking water. The Communist rebuilding of the country promised to provide improved living conditions. And the reforms made by Deng Xiaoping promised prosperity, or outright wealth. The struggles of 100 million poverty-stricken citizens is posing serious ethical and economic questions for China today.

Chinese authorities are not blind to their country's growing difficulties. The exploitation of land and resources has been visibly devastating to the country. There has been a newfound emphasis on harnessing wind power, developing solar panels, and exploring other sources of sustainable energy. But the emphasis on China

DID YOU KNOW

For years, the Harvard Business School has offered a course called Doing Business in China. The course is designed to prepare students "for a lifetime of inescapable engagement with China."

as an export power is not expected to change any time soon. Exports truly are the foundation of China's economy, with crucial social underpinnings. Tens of millions of rural residents have moved to the cities in search of work. The government, perennially afraid of mass revolt, wants to avoid upheaval at the hands of the disaffected unemployed, and has done everything in its power to facilitate these mass relocations.

At the same time, environmental damage has reached epidemic proportions. The gap between the haves and have-nots is an ever-widening chasm. For any regime, these are ominous indicators. For this vast land with its strong Marxist-Leninist heritage, the contradictions pose serious challenges. Mao did not envision sweatshops and workers unable to organize or to secure adequate health and safety standards.

In certain cases, the mistreatment of Chinese factory workers is brutal. China Labor Watch reported widespread instances of workers making "just over a dollar an hour, nowhere near a living wage. Many live in cramped company dormitories with inadequate bathroom facilities." The consequences reach far beyond China's borders. The consumer advocate Ralph Nader wrote that, today, nearly 85 percent of children's toys sold in the United States are China-manufactured. The toys "often come with too many hazards—burning, choking risks for small children, or toxins in or on the toys.... A singing monkey toy, sold in Cracker Barrel restaurants, has a battery compartment that can overheat and cause burns.... a Hello Kitty whistle, distributed by McDonald's" contains a "small internal piece [that] can come detached and be swallowed or choked on by young users." Safety concerns about products from China can often have a widespread effect. Until these grievous safety violations are addressed, Chinese manufacturing faces a confidence crisis.

> *The government, perennially afraid of mass revolt, wants to avoid upheaval at the hands of the disaffected unemployed.*

Prosperity is the new legitimacy on which the People's Republic rests. When there are holes in the prosperity of China, the repercussions can be graver than in other parts of the world. Slower economic growth and severe downturns are a challenge to Beijing. Improvement in infrastructure is largely controlled by local governments. If the economy is sagging, revenue for local governments decreases. These consequences are not confined to China, but their impact is especially felt by Chinese workers. And then, one must factor in China's lack of arable land and a massive, ever-growing population. No other government has to grapple with the wellbeing of a 1.3 billion-strong population. China's geographic size and multitude of regions is logistically unwieldy for a centralized government. Rebellion and revolts can spread and gain popular appeal.

Beijing is well aware of its critics. This is not the era of the underground, antigovernment pamphlet, smuggled illegally from hand to hand. With Facebook and Twitter, China is growing ever more connected to the rest of the world. French cars aren't the only thing imported into China; so are notions of freedom of assembly, representative government, unfettered expression and political pluralism.

Pinning a regime's hopes on the fluctuations of the global economy is a hazardous sport. In January 2015, Kaisa, a huge Chinese real estate group, defaulted on a $500 million debt owed to foreign creditors. For a government so tied to economic triumphalism, these are dangerous developments. Bubbles burst, economic booms collapse; and often they do.

China is poised on the edge of undisputed global economic dominance, but with warning lights flashing all along the way. The country faces demographic challenges and a growing threat to its authoritarian politics. The whole world has an interest in how things will turn out.

FOUR GREAT INVENTIONS

CHINA'S WORLD-CHANGING FIRSTS

Paper is a Chinese invention that dates to the 2nd century BCE. The oldest known paper sample was dated between 140 and 87 BCE. Paper reached India hundreds of years later, in the 7th century.

Gunpowder was invented in the 9th century. It was first described in a Chinese chronicle from 1044.

The compass is a Chinese invention from the 4th century BCE. Those compasses pointed south, which the Chinese considered the most significant cardinal direction.

Fixed-type, engraved printing is an innovation from 7th-century China. Eventually this was developed into a workable clay typeface.

A CHOKED NATION

THE AIRPOCALYPSE

I n 2015 journalist Chai Jing released a documentary in China. *Under the Dome* investigated the growing peril of air pollution, a crippling problem in many parts of China. She undertook the project for personal reasons: after becoming pregnant, she grew concerned over the future health of her child. *Under the Dome* protested the flimsiness of emissions controls in China, and environmental regulations as a whole. The film was made with input from governmental agencies, but it was suddenly pulled from websites. The media was instructed to avoid any mention of *Under the Dome*. But this was after 200 million people had already watched it.

The Chinese government has been extraordinarily sensitive about the serious environmental damage happening under its watch. It is not just urban pollution: Rural areas have been choked with industrial output as well. An estimated 600 million Chinese are breathing polluted air. Some urban areas report 25 smoggy days a month, constituting a near-permanent condition. Water has been contaminated on a mass scale: nearly 500 million Chinese do not have reliable access to safe drinking water.

Right: Pedestrians walk past a stone statue of Mao Zedong in heavy smog in Shenyang, in northeast China's Liaoning Province.

The World Heath Organization (WHO) measures pollution using a rate of 10 micrograms per cubic meter of pollutants. A highly polluted American city—Bakersfield, California—is measured at 18.2; Xingtai, one of the most polluted Chinese cities, comes in at 155.2. About 560 million Chinese people live in urban areas, and only 1 percent breathe clean air, as defined by the European Union.

Chinese officials oscillate between candor and cover-up. Wang Anshun, the mayor of Beijing, has described his city's pollution as a "life-or-death situation," and has deemed Beijing unlivable. *Under the Dome*, prior to being yanked from circulation, did receive some official support. Air-quality data can't be hidden. Nor can the dramatic rise in cancer rates, resulting from rampant pollution. Internationally, China's pollution causes acid rain in Tokyo and Seoul. Even some of the air pollution in Los Angeles originates in China. The government has launched initiatives to enforce restrictions on industrial pollution, and to limit the number of cars that are choking China's roads, and its drivers. The health costs of the environmental catastrophes are rising, and there is danger that the government may be perceived as poisoning its own citizens. But what the government announces and what it actually does can be two different things.

The Chinese government defends itself with the argument that the rest of the world is complicit and shares in the blame, whilst Europe and the United States keep reaping the benefits from the flood of low-cost Chinese goods.

CHINA IN THE LEAD

1 **China** has the world's largest population. With more than 1.3 billion people, it makes up 20 percent of the planet's entire population.

2 **Chinese drivers** on average travel greater distances than drivers in any other nation.

3 **The most** common language in the world is Mandarin.

4 **China** has the world's largest high-speed rail network.

5 **China** has the world's largest standing army. The United States' is second.

6 **China's Grand Canal** is the longest and oldest canal in the world, at more than 1,000 miles.

7 **China** leads the world in the number of state-sanctioned executions.

8 **China** is number one in the production of air conditioners, mobile phones, personal computers, and shoes.

FEEDING THE FUTURE

HOW WILL THE IMPORT OF WESTERN TASTES AFFECT THE FOOD SUPPLY?

Although by no means unique to Chinese industrialization, food production, supply, and safety are rising concerns, as China enters a new global chapter. Upton Sinclair's novel *The Jungle*, written in the early 20th century presents a shocking account of worker oppression and unsanitary practices in the industrial production of food in the United States. China is up against a similar crisis.

Chinese consumption of meat has tripled since the 1980s, which represents a seismic shift in agricultural production. Crops that are food for cattle and chickens are now cultivated on a massive scale.

> *Chinese consumption of meat has tripled since the 1980s, which represents a seismic shift in agricultural production.*

Food-processing plants and factories are ridden with conditions that wouldn't be unfamiliar to the readers of *The Jungle*. When a strong overlay of official corruption is added, the results become even more devastating: Baby formula in China has been linked to mass illness and deaths; food and water contamination are rampant; diseased pork, tainted eggs, and mislabeled meat all make it to market. A quality-control group that carried out widespread inspections of factories and processing plants found that half the food in production did not meet acceptable food-safety guidelines.

China faces two opposite, equally damaging, forces when it comes to food. One, is a powerful, unresponsive government that is corrupt and disinclined to change. The other, is that, in many cases, government agencies are too weak to challenge the system. Well-intended attempts to enact reforms have been ineffective in China's food-supply chain.

In 2005 the book *The China Study* shot to the bestseller list, with sales figures nearing 1 million copies. The book examined plant-based diets of Taiwan and rural China and was touted by Bill Clinton as the key to his weight loss. It was a positive spotlight on more traditional Chinese diets, and a condemnation of the increasing consumption of large amounts of meat and dairy—a.k.a. the Standard American Diet. By importing the Western preference for meat-heavy diets, China is also opting for the consequences they bring. Not only does meat production require the land, water, and resources to raise and slaughter the animals, but in a country where the lack of oversight has repeatedly brought unsafe foods to market, a greater demand for meat allows for even more opportunity of a modern-day Jungle.

Self-interest will likely spur reforms. Citizens cite food concerns with increasing urgency. And China does not wish to be synonymous with unsafe food, for reasons to do with both prosperity and national pride.

FEMINISM IN CHINA

OF ACTIVISTS AND AGGRESSORS

L ike the rest of China's multifaceted cultural history, attitudes toward women have also been complicated. Although there has been a number of standout icons, women have suffered the injustices of patriarchy in China just as they have in other parts of the world.

The People's Republic of China strove, in some ways, to do away with these gender prejudices. The Communist Party actively admitted women to their ranks, and outlawed the sale of brides, and the practices of child marriage and prostitution, as well as the use of concubines. By 1949, the custom of women undergoing foot-binding was already dwindling, but this too was explicitly outlawed. For the first time in the country's

Above: Protesters in Hong Kong fight for gender equality.

history, women were able to partake in state-sponsored education, and there was state-funded child care. The Communists promised emancipation. Women were largely expected to conform to the image of the male proletariat: tough, rugged, and patriotic. After Mao's Great Leap Forward, it is estimated that around 90 percent of the country's women started earning wages. But when the same movement brought significant economic and social hardship, it was the same women who were urged to return to the home and assume traditional roles.

Even a significant regime change, like the one in 1949, couldn't undo centuries of institutional and cultural gender bias. And, now, there is virulent discrimination emerging in China's headlong rush to capitalism, which is concentrated predominantly in turning a profit, rather than addressing social issues. Women now have less control over their financial assets, and are steadily losing ground in the pay scale compared to men. Institutional and workplace sexism are rampant. Some jobs are explicitly advertised as men-only, or open only to attractive women. China is again seeing a rise in prostitution, human trafficking, sexual harassment, assault, and the pernicious components of a sexist culture that many thought was a thing of the past.

In the late 1970s, the government implemented a family planning policy that harshly penalized couples for having too many children. (It has become widely known as the one-child policy, which is not altogether accurate; some families can and do have more than one child.) This policy of limiting family size made many parents reluctant to "waste" their allotted number of children on a daughter, creating a dramatic rise of female infanticide. The introduction of ultrasound and other methods to detect a baby's sex means that abortion of baby-girls-to-be has become widespread.

Currently, there are active and inspired feminists throughout China, though they face a particularly steep uphill battle. In just one example from early 2015, a group of five women planned to hand out stickers protesting domestic violence for International Women's Day. Wang Man, Zheng Churan, Wu Rongrong, Wei Tingting, and Li Tingting were arrested and jailed for more than a month, simply for *planning* a demonstration. They were freed after a wave of international media attention and entreaties from the United States and European Union for their release. Just as they do in most of the world, feminists in China struggle with the disparity between formal and actual equality. The major problem this new wave of activists faces is the same any other activist in China has to deal with: a regime that does not take kindly to dissent.

CHINESE DREAM

DREAM

THE RISE OF XI JINPING

China's current leader, Xi Jinping, rose to the top in 2012. He is a different sort of leader from the technocrats of the post-Deng era, a return to the outsized Chinese rulers and the personality cults. Papa Xi, as he is affectionately known, caused a sensation when he stopped at a Beijing fast-food restaurant, paid for his order out of his own pocket, and unceremoniously took his tray to one of the eatery's folding tables. Bold, charming, and larger-than-life, Xi declared that his rule would be undergirded by what he called the "Chinese Dream"—"the great rejuvenation of the Chinese nation," he said. This stood in direct contrast to the leaders who came before him. His immediate predecessor, Hu Jintao governed—with perfect Communist-era technocratic dullness—under the slogan "Scientific Outlook on Development."

Xi expounded on his Chinese Dream, encapsulating China's goal as the "Two 100s." The first means eliminating economic inequity by 2021—the 100th anniversary of the Chinese Communist Party. The second, is to become a truly developed nation by 2049: the 100th anniversary of the founding of the People's Republic. One-party rule under Xi is a critical element of the plan.

The idea of the Chinese Dream has admittedly been played up in China; the phrase itself has become part of the parlance. There are four main tenets of the Chinese Deam, as put forth by Xi Jinping: Strong China, Civilized China, Harmonious China, and Beautiful China. Taken together, these amount to China developing as a cohesive, modern nation—one that continually advances in politics, health, science, diplomacy, and quality of life for its citizens.

The Chinese Dream, of course, invites comparisons to the American

Dream. The idealized American Dream is a prime example of language inflation. Historically, entire segments of American society have been left out of this dream. Can China realize its national dream, or are the goals too lofty for any nation—and especially one of China's size—to actually accomplish?

China, by the broad strokes of what defines a middle class, certainly has one: By Chinese estimates, 300 million people fall into the middle class, a number that may very well double in the next few decades.

The shadow of political instability and an absolute aversion to dissent haunts the Chinese leadership. There has been no letup on official control of various social media; Facebook, YouTube, and Twitter have all fallen out of favor with officials. The Chinese Dream, therefore, comes with a definite political overlay.

Xi Jinping is a bold, assertive leader who wishes for a bold, assertive China. There has also been a new assertiveness in territorial disputes with India, Japan, and other Southeast Asian countries. China's neighbors are powers in their own right, and even those that lack a strong military presence—like South Korea and Taiwan—are economic powerhouses. China will not be able to dominate its sphere of influence the way the Soviet Union did in Eastern Europe.

This new, full-throttle official push toward the Chinese Dream definitely has many complicated, contradictory factors. The Chinese Dream has been paired with the idea of a massive national revival. As China has shed so much of its Marxist underpinnings, there is also a definite shift back to the perceived glories of the past: the era when the Communist Party of Mao Zedong threw off China's colonialist shackles and made the country a force to be reckoned with.

Deputies attend the second plenary meeting of the Third Session of the 12th National People's Congress at the Great Hall of the People in Beijing.

The fact that so much of its economic power comes from being an export power, means China lacks any sort of economic infrastructure that can absorb a global downturn. The global economy can turn with startling speed. And for all of China's economic might, it has a difficult time providing for the needs of hundreds of millions of its citizens.

Will China mark the passing of the Two 100s as a nation collectively enjoying the realization of the Chinese Dream? As all presidents do, Xi Jinping inherited the legacies of his predecessors. In Xi's case, his work is weaving together the identities of three fairly distinct Chinas: the dynastic monolith, Mao's republic, and today's China—the emerging superpower.

A PARTING THOUGHT

"When the wind of change blows, some build walls while others build windmills."

—LI KEQIANG, PREMIER OF THE PEOPLE'S REPUBLIC OF CHINA

BIBLIOGRAPHY

Asia for Educators, Columbia University. afe.easia.columbia.edu/main_pop/kpct/kp_ming.htm

Bhattacharji, Preeti. "Religion in China." Council on Foreign Relations. May 16, 2008. www.cfr.org/china/religion-china/p16272

Bernstein, Richard. *China 1945: Mao's Revolution and America's Fateful Choice.* New York: Knopf, 2014.

Binyan, Liu, with Ruan Ming and Xu Gang. *"Tell the World": What Happened in China and Why.* Translated by Henry L. Epstein. New York: Random House, 1989.

"Chiang Kai-shek: Chinese Statesman," Encyclopedia Britanica. www.britannica.com/EBchecked/topic/110142/Chiang-Kai-shek#ref216154

Chang, Jung, and Jon Halliday. *Mao: The Unknown Story.* New York: Knopf, 2005.

Fairbank, John King. *China: A New History.* Cambridge, MA: The Belknap Press of Harvard University Press, 1992.

Hewitt, Duncan. *China: Getting Rich First.* New York: Pegasus Books, 2008.

Hickman, Kennedy. "Second Opium War: Overview." militaryhistory.about.com/od/battleswars1800s/p/secondopiumwar.htm

Kristof, Nicholas D. "China's Future on Hold with a 'Gang of Elders.'" *New York Times.* June 3, 1990. www.nytimes.com/1990/06/03/world/china-s-future-on-hold-with-a-gang-of-elders.html.

Kristof, Nicholas D., and Sheryl WuDunn. *China Wakes: The Struggle for the Soul of a Rising Power.* New York: Times Books, 1994.

Lifton, Robert Jay. *Revolutionary Immortality: Mao Tse-tung and the Chinese Cultural Revolution.* New York: Random House, 1968.

Long-hsuen, Hsu, and Chang Ming-kai. *The History of the Sino-Japanese War (1937–1945).* Translated by Wen Ha-hsiung. Taipei, Taiwan: Chung Wu Publishing Company, 1971.

"Little Man in a Big Hurry." *Time* magazine. January 1, 1979.

"Milestones: 1899–1913." US Dept. of State, Office of the Historian. history.state.gov/milestones/1899-1913/chinese-rev

Nader, Ralph. "Toys from Abusive Chinese Factories Bring No Holiday Cheer." *CounterPunch.* December 23, 2014. www.counterpunch.org/2014/12/23/toys-from-abusive-chinese-factories-bring-no-holiday-cheer/.

"Opium Wars." Encyclopedia Britanica. www.britannica.com/EBchecked/topic/430163/Opium-Wars

Pan, Philip P. *Out of Mao's Shadow: The Struggle for the Soul of a New China.* New York: Simon & Schuster, 2008.

Reporters Without Borders: World Press Freedom Index 2014. rsf.org
/index2014/en-index2014.php.

Salisbury, Harrison E. *China: 100 Years of Revolution*. New York: Holt,
Rhinehart and Winston, 1983.

Schell, Orville, and John Delury. *Wealth and Power: China's Long March to the
Twenty-first Century*. New York: Random House, 2013.

Spence, Jonathan. *The Search for Modern China*. New York: W.W. Norton, 1990.

Tatlow, Didi Kirsten, and Michael Forsythe. "In China's Modern Economy,
a Retro Push Against Women." *New York Times*. February 20, 2015.
nytimes.com/2015/02/21/world/asia/china-women-lag-in-work-force
-especially-in-top-jobs.html.

"The Qing Dynasty." China Highlights, www.chinahighlights.com
/travelguide/china-history/the-qing-dynasty.htm

Tse-tung, Mao. *The Poems of Mao Tse-tung*. Translated by Willis Barstone
and Ko Ching-po. New York: Harper & Row, 1972.

Tyler, Patrick. "Deng Xiaoping: A Political Wizard Who Put China on the
Capitalist Road." *New York Times*. February 20, 1997. nytimes.com
/learning/general/onthisday/bday/0822.html.

van Schaik, Sam. *Tibet: A History. Yale University Press. New Haven: 2013.*

Weiwei, Ai. "Why I'll Stay Away from the Opening Ceremony of the
Olympics." *The Guardian*. August 7, 2008. www.theguardian.com
/commentisfree/2008/aug/07/olympics2008.china.

www.cia.gov/library/publications/the-world-factbook/geos/ch.html

www.nature.org/ourinitiatives/regions/asiaandthepacific/china
/placesweprotect/china-yangtze-river.xml.

www.nytimes.com/2007/08/26/world/asia/26china.html?
pagewanted=all&_r=0.

Xiaobo, Liu. *No Enemies, No Hatred: Selected Essays and Poems*. Cambridge,
MA: The Belknap Press of Harvard University Press, 2012.

INDEX

CONTINUE THE
CONVERSATION

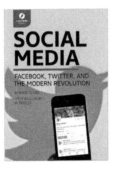

SOCIAL MEDIA
FACEBOOK, TWITTER, AND THE MODERN REVOLUTION

CROWD-SOURCING
AIRBNB, KICKSTARTER, UBER AND THE DISTRIBUTED ECONOMY

WILL PLATFORMS KILL THE CORPORATION?
YOUR ARE THE SHARING ECONOMY

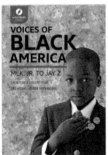

VOICES OF BLACK AMERICA
MLK, JR. TO JAY Z

MARS
SCIENCE FICTION TO COLONIZATION

CUBA
CASTRO, REVOLUTION, AND THE END OF THE EMBARGO

DISCOVER MORE AT
www.lightningguides.com/books

Also available as an eBook

CPSIA information can be obtained at www.ICGtesting.com
Printed in the USA
BVOW11s1602140615

404496BV00006B/6/P